S0-FQW-013

Brandon –

God bless you!

Dee Stone

Experiencing GRACE

One woman's year long
journey with God after the
death of her mother

Dee Stone

Experiencing GRACE
One Woman's Year Long Journey with God after the death of her mother

by
D. Michelle Stokes

220 Publishing

Chicago, Illinois

220 Publishing
(A Division of 220 Communications)
Chicago

© 2010 by D. Michelle Stokes

All rights reserved. Printed and bound in the United States of America. No part of this book may be reproduced or transmitted in any form or by any means, electronic or mechanical, including photocopying, recording, or by any information storage or retrieval system except by a reviewer who may quote brief pages in a review to be printed in a magazine or newspaper, without written permission from the publisher and the author:

220 Publishing
(A Division of 220 Communications)
PO Box 8186
Chicago, IL 60680-8186
www.220communications.com
www.twitter.com/team220

First Edition
Printed in the United States

Cover Design : S. Teresa Brassel   steresa@hotmail.com

ISBN 978-1-4507-3582-7

Although the author and publisher have made every effort to ensure the accuracy and completeness of information contained in this book, we assume no responsibility for errors, inaccuracies, omissions or any inconsistency therein.
Any slights of people, places belief systems or organizations are unintentional. Any resemblance to any living, dead or somewhere in between is truly coincidental unless otherwise noted. All living persons referenced in this book are used with permission granted to the author.

Dedication

This book is dedicated to the most influential person ever to come into my earthly life: my mother, nurturer, biggest fan, and soror Ernestine W. Gibson. I can't wait to see you again...enjoy Heaven!

Acknowledgements

There are so many wonderful people I should mention who were instrumental in supporting me throughout this time. Some are mentioned in the book. I first need to thank my family. To my stepdad and brother who are still hurting after our loss. I love you guys and wish God's GRACE upon each of you. To my aunts, cousins, dad, brothers and sisters. Thanks for the phone calls, cards, and prayers. I love and appreciate all of you more than you will ever know. Special thanks to Ed Baldwin for calling me everyday for a solid two week period. I wish I would have been more supportive to you when your father passed, but I was still messed up. I love you! Thanks to Kwamine Washington Simpson, my dearest friend on this earth, for quite simply: EVERYTHING! Lastly, thanks to my brother and publisher Glenn Murray who put up with me and my demands during the publishing of this book. Glenn, you are so special and I am glad God saw fit to make us siblings! You mean more to me than I can explain. God bless you in your future endeavors.

Table of Contents

Foreword

*"Trust in the Lord with all your heart and lean not on
your own understanding; in all your ways acknowledge
Him, and He shall direct your path."
– Proverbs 3:5-6 (NKJV)*

"GRACE"

May 27, 2009

Our lives are anointed. Anwar Sadat, once ruler of Israel
said, "my life is anointed and I shall not live one day longer
or die one day sooner than I am supposed to." My mother
died on Tuesday May 12, 2009 . . . yes, only a few days
ago. Only by His Grace am I able to write these words. We
are still somewhat uncertain about why my mom took a
turn for the worse. She had been sick for about a month and
then a week after gallbladder surgery, she was gone. When
I heard the news last Tuesday, I was angry because I did
not know how she died. I never questioned why though.
You see, my grandmother died a little over a year ago – in
March of 2008 – so the two most influential women in my
life are gone from this earth . . . leaving me here to live on
in their legacies. My life is anointed and during the last
year, God and His Holy Spirit have been moving and
working in me in ways I had not even imagined until now.
I have had an encounter with the Holy Spirit that has
changed me forever and I will not be the same again. The
following is a record of the ways God has shown up and
moved in my life to bless me throughout the last year. He
was preparing me for this time in my life.

1) I have had five friends lose a parent in the last year. Four
of those lost their dads and one lost his mother. I tried to

console them, but I did not really know how . . . now I know how.

2) I started taking classes on May 11th , but I really *started* about a week and a half before that. I thought it was my anal retentiveness that drove me to start early, but it was God, pushing me to finish my work ahead of time and turn in all of my assignments before the classes officially began on the 11th - the week of my mother's death. So last week, I did no studying at all because it had all been done.

3) And check this out . . . in one of my classes, we were to read Proverbs 1-3 for the first week's assignment. For you that are familiar with this passage of scripture, you know that in Proverbs – the 3rd chapter, it reads, "Lean not unto thy own understanding, in all thy ways acknowledge Him and He will direct your path." God was speaking to me through this passage of scripture and I had no idea until now! Wow! How powerful is He? Our small minds cannot even fathom the infinite wisdom of God!

4) I spoke to my mom for the last time on Mother's Day. God let her live through that day and I distinctly remember – along with a friend of mine – telling her I loved her. Some folks don't get a chance to do that before their loved ones pass away.

5) God placed on my heart several months ago these words: *Dee Stokes Ministries, "A Worship Experience," Song, Prayer, Devotion . . .* and I got a chance to speak at an FCA (Fellowship of Christian Athletes) meeting the Monday before my mom died. I am continuing to ask God to show me what to do with *Dee Stokes Ministries.*

6) I have been praying over a four or five week span now for my family. I had been praying for jobs lost and good health for them. You see, my ex sister- in- law has no job,

my brother is still struggling, my aunt is losing her job on June 1st and my uncle has Stage IV cancer. I'd thought that I was praying for these things, but now the Spirit has revealed to me that I was actually praying for strength and I did not even know it . . . strength for us to get through this time.

7) Every time I heard my mom's group, the Arkansas Mass Choir, sing their song, "I Lift My Hands" on XM radio (by the way, I can't live without XM – how about you? LOL), I would just lift my hands anywhere I was, even in the car and I would be so proud that my mom sang with that group. I told almost everyone about it.

8) I was supposed to be on vacation this week – the week of May 18th. I had planned to go to Puerto Rico, but cancelled my trip to use the ticket to go to Arkansas instead and I have since been in Tennessee with a friend. God knew that I needed this week to relax and heal.

9) You will get a kick out of this one . . . LOL . . . God is so good that on Sunday, May 10th (Mother's Day), I did not sleep all night. Sometimes I play meetings over and over again in my head and I did have that FCA meeting on Monday the 11th, but that is not what kept me up that night. I was thinking about a trip I was supposed to make to D.C. on Monday night for a meeting on Tuesday morning. I had no idea until now, why I grappled with it so much and eventually woke up Monday morning and decided not to go. I remember telling my staff in a meeting that I was not going because I didn't need to drive, didn't have anywhere to stay and had too much going on. On Tuesday, after I arrived safely into the parking lot at work (I was not driving) I received the call about my mom. God blessed me to not be on the road and to not even be driving when I got the call . . . He is blessing me for some extraordinary reason! As the songwriter wrote, "Where would I be if not for your Grace? Carrying me in every season. Where

would I be if not for your Grace? You came to my rescue and I want to thank you for your Grace!"

My mother's death has shocked me to the core and I will never be the same again, BUT every time (you know we are selfish by nature and care way too much about ourselves) I start to be selfish and have thoughts of how I can't believe I will never see you again or you left me – what will I do now . . . the Holy Spirit moves throughout me, breathes a breath of fresh air into my lungs, I soak it in with a deep breath and the faucet of tears is turned off. Just when I needed Him the most He stepped in. He walks and sits beside me . . . I can feel His presence constantly. He is guiding me through typing this passage. I could go on and tell you so many more ways God has blessed me, but the underlying theme here is that He is BLESSING little 'ole me. I don't know what His plans are for me exactly, but I know "His plans are to prosper me." I am more convicted than ever to seek His face and His Will for my life. My mother was a Godly woman who loved God and taught us how to love Him. We had a great example for our lives. I want to honor her with how I live my life for God. I am dedicated to that. Thank you Lord for your "Grace."

Introduction

"Yea, though I walk through the valley of the shadow of death, I will fear no evil; for though art with me; thy rod and thy staff, they comfort me."
– Psalm 23:4 (NKJV)

I wrote the passage, "Grace" just a few days after the death of my mother. The year I lost my mother was 2009. To be exact, it was May 12, 2009. I remember that day as if it were yesterday. After I had safely arrived at work, I received a call from my stepdad who, by the way, never called me . . . "Your mom passed," he exclaimed. Those words still reverberate in my soul. I cannot get those words out of my head. That day is still so vivid. My staff was by my side along with a co-worker, as I called many friends and family members. I even called a childhood friend whose birthday was that day, but not with birthday well wishes. My dear friend Kwamine drove from Columbia, SC to Winston-Salem, NC in break-neck time to be by my side that day. I cannot express my gratitude to her for being such a great friend. I love you my sister.

The next few days are a blur, but I remember the very Spirit-filled service for my mother. My mom was an activist, actress, singer and dedicated Alpha Kappa Alpha woman. She was a member of one church for 33 years and one sorority for over 35 years. She was special and someone once said she was bigger than life. Her funeral was so big that it had to be held at my former high school in Fayetteville, AR. The very floor where I made my name as a basketball player is where we celebrated the life of my biggest fan. It was just as she would have wanted it. Most who saw her for the last time noticed a smile on her face as she was laid to rest. Rest in peace Ernestine White Gibson! You are sorely missed!

Since beginning this book, more tragedy has come in my life. My paternal grandfather died about two weeks after my mother, my beloved uncle (Mom's brother) succumbed to cancer in August and an ex-boyfriend of mine died suddenly in Charlotte at the age of 43 the same month. Later this year in February, my great uncle (maternal grandmother's brother) died from a long battle with cancer. God is still on the throne and He is still in control . . . praise His Holy name!

This book is meant to be an inspirational one. It will be sad, but it is intended to show how, through God's mercy and grace and through an unwavering faith in Christ, YOU can overcome any heartache in your life even when you think you can't. This book does not just pertain to losses of life in your world, but it can apply to losing a job or yourself in your family or career.

Too often we lose ourselves and we do not know how to deal with those types of losses. Truthfully, they can be more devastating at times than losing a loved one. I lost myself in my career, but God stuck with me and woke me up one day to let me know that it doesn't matter what your career choice is, "I just want to love you and be in relationship with you." What a blessing! This book will cover a full year of my life after my mother's death. It will document my journey from May 12, 2009 to May 12, 2010. My prayer is that it inspires you to keep on moving forward and to never look back. Be blessed!

HE IS ALL WE NEED!

Why does God take the most precious things from us during the times that we feel like we need them the most? So that we will understand that God is ALL WE NEED! Also, so we will learn to lean and depend on the King of Kings and the Lord of Lords and NOT on man. Man cannot provide us with what we need.

All my life God, you have been my Father when my father was not around and now you are my Mother because my earthly mother is now with you. When I was broke, I never missed a meal. Thank you! When they repossessed my car, I still had another car to drive. Thank you! When I couldn't afford to pay rent or a mortgage, I still had a roof over my head and I never spent one night homeless. Thank you! You step in right on time, just when we need you the most. You provide the things we need and sometimes what we want . . . when we think those things are important . . . even though they really aren't. God, thank you for being ALL WE NEED!

CHAPTER 1

"My brethren, count it all joy when you fall into various trials, knowing that the testing of your faith produces patience."
–James 1: 2-3 (NKJV)

TWO YEAR
CAREER BATTLE

I remember it so well. It was May 6, 2007 when God spoke to me in a mighty way. I was at my church, Winston-Salem First Assembly of God and I don't quite remember what Pastor Rakes was preaching about, but the Holy Spirit started moving in me very strongly. I began to weep and could not stop crying. I composed myself long enough to leave church, but immediately, when I got into my car, I began to weep more than ever. I did not even know what to say or think. I felt like I was having some "out- of-body" experience. As I drove to Greensboro to get some-thing to eat, all I could think about was buying some new dishes. Then, after driving down the highway aimlessly, God showed me the "*#1*." I tried so hard for two years to figure out what that number meant. I thought it meant one more year in Winston-Salem and then I would move again. I thought it meant one more year and then God would show me a new and different path. Not until the summer of 2009 did I know what that "#1" meant. I now believe it was God's hand showing His index finger and telling me to wait. The Bible says, "Wait on the Lord, be of good courage and He will strengthen your heart, wait I say on the Lord" (Psalm 27:14). I thought for two years that I was in a battle with God over retiring from coaching, but the battle was to understand what He wanted for me. In His perfect Will for my life, He was telling me to wait on Him, be patient, and He will show me the path. God sure did that for me and in the summer of 2009, I told everyone that the 2009-2010 season would be my last as a collegiate coach. I did not tell people that this was my decision, but that God had *told* me to retire. That may not be necessarily true either. I now understand that God just wants to be close to me no matter what I do. What I now know is that God has given me wisdom on my finances, how to search for positions, and how to listen to Him when He speaks. He has given me so many ideas of things to do this year and I am truly grateful. During the 2008-2009 season I wanted to quit, but God knew it was not the time. You see He was preparing me for the personal losses that I faced in 2009 as well as for a career change. God is good and if you are in His will, you will live life abundantly.

Have you ever had an "ah-ha" moment in your life? That moment for me came one Wednesday night in February of 2010 when I was at a church service. I call "ah-ha" moments, revelations of sorts and since I have surrendered to God, I have lots of them. It took me 37 years to finally listen for His voice and 40 years to truly understand His Will for my life. As my pastor put it that Wednesday night, God's Will for our lives is not a job, career, person, place or thing. God's Will for our lives is to have an intimate relationship with us and that whatever we do, we should do it to glorify Him. That hit me like a brick right there in the pew of First Assembly.

It seems that ever since May of 2007, my relationship with Christ has gotten so much better and so intimate and the closer we became, the less I wanted to coach. The more I cared about disciplining and educating kids, the less I cared about wins and losses. Wins and losses don't define us as coaches. Let me type that one again; WINS AND LOSSES DON'T DEFINE US AS COACHES! That is a word in itself for someone reading this book right now. You are so much more than the number of wins you have or the bank account you possess or the million dollar deals that you close. You are a child of the most high King. You will inherit the biggest Kingdom of them all . . . streets paved with gold. I can't wait to see Heaven. No matter what your position (career) in life, God wants to have a relationship with you. Do the best you can and be the best at whatever you decide to do. You decide what job makes you happy, then go after it and do well for the Kingdom. That is God's Will for our lives.

CHAPTER 2

"Make a joyful shout to the Lord, all you lands! Serve the Lord with gladness; come before His presence with singing. Know that the Lord, He is God; it is He who has made us, and not we ourselves; we are His people and the sheep of His pasture. Enter into His gates with thanksgiving, and into His courts with praise. Be thankful to Him, and bless His name. For the Lord is good; His mercy is everlasting, and His truth endures to all generations."
—Psalm 100 (NKJV)

IT IS OK
TO ASK FOR HELP

From May 12th to about December of 2009, I tried to go about grieving on my own. Don't get me wrong, God gave me so much grace, mercy, and showed kindness through it all, but I felt like no one around me understood what was going on. I thought that no one cared. How could people just pass by me and say nothing? Didn't they know what I was going through? Didn't my staff, co-workers, church members, and players understand? Why didn't they show more concern? No one understood what I was going through. They did not and no one can truly understand until they experience such a loss.

To those of you reading this book, I really want you to get this chapter. It was the hardest thing for me to do during the toughest time in my life. In December of 2009, I finally asked for professional help. I had reached a point where I could no longer go home at night by myself and continue to suffer the way I was. No one, absolutely no one, knew what I was going through. At least two or more times per week, I would just sit in my house and cry. I could no longer continue to cry every night and feel the way I felt. I decided to just go online and look up a psychiatric facility. I was not crazy and everyone who goes to one of these places is not crazy. I was grieving – plain and simple.

I met with a grief counselor and she helped me immediately. She shared some things with me about her personal experience with losing her own mother, how to cope during the holidays and how she felt the first time her stepdad had another woman in the house where her mother had once resided. She gave me some literature to read so that I could get through my first Christmas without my mom. I did and I felt really good because I made it through! Seek help if you need it and DO NOT be ashamed!

CHAPTER 3

"He who dwells in the secret place of the Most High shall abide under the shadow of the Almighty. I will say of the Lord, He is my refuge and my fortress; my God, in Him I will trust."
—Psalm 91: 1-2 (NKJV)

THE BAHAMAS

I want to make you laugh and cry at the same time with this chapter. I want to show you how God moves in your life. God can do anything He wants to do and He can show up, influence and use any person, place or thing He wants to use for His glory. He used my trip to the Bahamas in August and a book entitled *The Shack*, by William P. Young to touch and heal me.

This trip was one that my mother and I had planned together. She and I were so excited about it and after her death, I contemplated whether to go or not. God started moving even before I took the trip. I tried frantically to find someone to go along with me, but to no avail. Now I know that the reason for this was so that I could spend my time alone with God each evening.

This book, *The Shack*, had been in my possession, just sitting on my book shelf since May. A friend of mine who had lost his dad earlier in the school year, had given it to me. I let it sit there for months. While I was recruiting in July, a former colleague of mine suggested I go and buy this book, *The Shack*. I thought that was odd and told him that I already owned the book, but had not read it yet. He asked me what I was waiting for. I promised him that I would read it while on my vacation in the Bahamas.

I started to read the book and the next few accounts will show you how God's hand was in the mix and at work. On the flight to Fort Lauderdale, I sat by the cutest couple with their baby. The wife looked over at me and said, "I see you are reading The Shack." I told her, "yes, it seems to be a book about healing and I just recently lost my mom." She said, "Oh . . . that must be why my mom is reading it

because we just recently lost my dad." Not thinking anything of it, I began to read more. The next day I was sitting
at the pool reading and a woman approached me and again
said, "I see you are reading The Shack." I said, "yes, it
seems to be a book about healing." She said, "I read it after
I lost my mom." I told her I had recently lost my mom.
Another God connection it seemed. Now this will blow
your mind. We boated over to the Bahamas. The ride was
about five hours or so and as I was leaving the boat, I met
a couple and we immediately hit it off. They were from
North Carolina, of all places and only lived about an hour
and a half from me. They were on their honeymoon and
guess what . . . you got it . . . the husband had lost his dad
about a year earlier. We said our goodbyes and I went to
my hotel which was quite far from the beach hotel where
they were staying. The hotel I was at (my mom had made
all of the arrangements) was a dump! I scattered to figure
out how to get out of that place and I remembered the name
of the hotel that most of the people on the boat were
staying at. I called and made a reservation . . . they laughed
when I told them where I was. I left the room, looked up to
Heaven, and said, "Mom . . . not such a good choice this
time, but I love you." When I got to the new hotel, the first
people I saw were the couple from North Carolina. The
husband looked at me, almost in tears and said his dad and
my mom were in Heaven planning this and knew we
needed to be together. For the rest of the week, we were
together every day. I spent every night reading **The Shack**
and spending time with God. I began to heal on that island
and for that, I am thankful.

For those who are considering reading **The Shack**, it is
about healing and about a man's encounter with God, Jesus
and the Holy Spirit at a shack. Some call it far-fetched, but
I believe God can do anything. He healed this man by
showing up. He will heal you if you invoke His presence
in your life. Just seek His face and ask Him for whatever
you want. He will give you the desires of your heart!

CHAPTER 4

"If a man dies, shall he live again? All the days of my hard service I will wait, till my change comes."
—Job 14:14 (NKJV)

DEATH AND DYING

Elizabeth Kubler-Ross (1969) acknowledges five stages in Death and Dying: Denial, Anger, Bargaining, Depression and Acceptance. These stages may or may not be appropriate for you, but I went through most of them more than once. It is important to know from the start that you may stay in one stage longer than the other, you may skip stages and you may repeat stages. I am writing this because I experienced this myself and not because I have studied Kubler-Ross to the extent to where I am a fan of hers. She did revolutionize grief and dying, but I am only writing on what I have experienced so that it will help you gain a better understanding.

Denial first began for me on the day when my stepdad called and said my mother had passed. Immediately my body went limp. I started screaming, but could not seem to cry. I then felt as if I could not breathe and that I was going to pass out. These are true bodily symptoms and maybe you have gone through these as well? I then went on for several months, not believing that this was true and questioning why. Denial can last quite a long time. To get through this stage, I had to pray for peace. "God grant me peace." It took some time, but God granted me what I asked for.

Anger is a dangerous emotion. I was so angry for months – not at God, but at the fact that we still did not know what really caused my mother's death. By the time I came to on May 12th they had already started preparing her body at the funeral home, so it was too late for an autopsy. I was angry because as a control freak, anal retentive person, I needed to know the facts and to understand the entire situation. During my angry stage, I found out many things too personal to share, but some gave me answers and others didn't which led me to stay angry for a while longer. I was still crying everyday and feeling lost. I was searching for answers. I even got my mother's medical records from her primary care physician – from March 2009 until her death. I am not a doctor, but I needed something to soothe me. I combed through those records, but had to put them aside one day. I needed to come back to them at another time, when my anger subsided. My brother and I even met with my mother's surgeon during the weekend of her funeral to get answers. We did not want to cause problems . . . we just needed the answers that we'd never gotten. I finally got out of this stage in about August of 2009, but many people may experience this stage for a much longer time.

I never went through the bargaining stage. I would never bargain with God for anything, but sometimes . . . I thought . . . I wished that I had died before my mother. Maybe that is bargaining? But, then I thought . . . I know how much my mother loved us all and it would have killed her to see one of her children die before her. She was just that loving.

I knew I was depressed when I couldn't focus the Tuesday before Thanksgiving 2009. I really knew I was depressed when after a game in December, my assistant coach came up to me to talk to me about my mood and habits. She felt something was wrong, but again she did not understand because she could pick up the phone and call her mother anytime she wanted. I then decided that I needed help. I had a dream one night several months earlier that I went into my closet and shot myself. At the time, I just so happened to have had a gun in the closet. Anyway, as I stated in an earlier chapter, it is okay to ask for help. Everyone who goes to a psychiatrist is not CRAZY. I met with a grief counselor who really helped me.

GO GET PROFESSIONAL HELP! Depression is a disease that you want to get rid of as soon as you can. You can do that without taking medication. I did so without taking medication.

Acceptance, for me, finally came about five or six months after my mother's death. I think it came with depression because I finally realized that she wasn't coming back. It was a hard thing to accept, but I did it and then sought help. Once you get to acceptance, you can move on with your life . . . one day at a time and one step forward at a time. A friend of mine once said, when she does something her mom told her not to do, she hears her mom's voice saying, "go shut off that dryer or clean up that closet." What is your mother saying to you right now? Ok mom!

CHAPTER 5

"For His anger is but for a moment, His favor is for life; weeping may endure for a night, but joy comes in the morning."
—Psalm 30:5 (NKJV)

THE PAIN

The pain of losing my mother cut and still cuts like a knife, even though I have accepted that she is not coming back. Just when you think you are getting better, you actually may go all the way back through the stages of Death & Dying. I still have trouble focusing on a picture of me and mom that is on my laptop. It was taken during the 2008 Centennial Boule of the Alpha Kappa Alpha Sorority, Inc.'s Legacy Dinner. It is just still so painful, but it is there as a reminder and to help me heal. Just when you stop crying everyday and maybe only cry once a week or every other week, there are times in your life when you just cry out, "I want my mom." I have gone through so many of those. When you wake up with good news, you want to call her. When you are having trouble making a decision, you want to call her. When you need that famous sweet potato pie recipe, you want to call her. There are so many instances when I just want to pick up the phone and call her.

Then, you compare her to everyone else in your life. The only thing my stepdad and me had in common was my mom. My father did not raise me, so the only person who truly knew me from birth and from the inside out, was my mother. When people do or don't do things, I often think, my mom would or wouldn't have done that. Even after eight or nine months of grieving, I still felt the pain and I still thought no one understood what I was going through. I am a rational person and realize that everyone has problems, but when one is hurting like this, you lose your sense of rationalism and reality.

Another remedy for pain is to share your story with others. I am doing that through this book. On Thursday February 25, 2010 I watched a movie entitled "Love Happens." It was not by chance. I had been thinking about a friend whose husband committed suicide back in 2006 and that led her to start writing books. On this very same day, I found one of her books and began to look through it which made me want to write her an e-mail . . . as I was writing the e-mail I put the movie in. To my surprise it was not a movie about "love" per se, but instead, it was a movie about healing. The main character had lost his wife in a car accident and how ironic is this, he wrote a book about it! However, he was teaching people at seminars who had lost loved ones about healing and dealing with loss, but he had never really dealt with his own loss. Call this irony or whatever you want, but I don't think things happen in this life by chance. My friend wrote a book after her loss, the movie was about a man who wrote a book after his loss and I am writing a book after my loss. Watch the movie; it has a healing quality.

When those tears start to well up in your eyes all of a sudden and it seems for no reason at all . . . just cry! Crying is another way of dealing with pain. All year long I have cried at the most inopportune times. I cry at the grocery store, in the car, before a game, on my way to church, getting on a plane. Just let those tears flow . . . it is your body's way of healing. Don't stop yourself from crying when you are grieving. Let it out. Don't let anyone tell you to be strong or not to show emotion. I don't care who you are – cry, cry, cry and make yourself feel better after you cry. Let it out and then get up and move on to the next task.

That deep dark place

Since my mother's death, I have found a place down deep within me that I never knew existed. I call it that deep, dark place. I cannot imagine that it would live in our souls because God lives there and where He is, there is nothing but goodness. I believe this place is deep down within our hearts and it is also in our minds. In this place, the Devil makes every attempt to dwell and tries to destroy us with pain, destruction, depression, desperation, exhaustion and on and on. I discovered that place this past year and I did not like it one bit. I recognized it early in this process of grieving and I have dealt with it positively ever since.

Don't let the Devil destroy you in this place. He gets in our hearts and in our thoughts and makes us think of crazy things in order to cope with our pain. Stop those thoughts right now in their tracks. Focus on the goodness of the Lord and everything will be fine. It will all work for your good.

CHAPTER 6

"That which is born of the flesh is flesh, and that which is born of the Spirit is spirit. Do not marvel that I said to you, You must be born again."
—John 3: 6-7 (NKJV)

MY BIRTHDAY

February 18, 1970 was my day of birth. I was born at 12:43 p.m. in Memphis, Tennessee to Ernestine White, a 17 year old West Memphis, Arkansas native. I'd thought that on February 18, 2010, my 40th birthday and the first birthday since my mother's death, I would be quite sad and depressed. I wasn't. The day started with homework on the computer, then more work on the computer and some service with the Piedmont Chamber Singers (a singing group with whom I served as a board member). The night ended with a friend of mine beating me at pool and plenty of laughing. Even though my stepdad had sang to me earlier that day and I'd heard the small faint voice of my mother in the background, I was not sad at all. You see, my mom and stepdad had sung to me on my birthday for as long as I can remember. I had a good day thanks to some good memories, good phone calls, gifts and the comfort of the Holy Spirit. My day ended early as most did and I slept very peacefully that night as a happy 40 year old. God is so good!

CHAPTER 7

"Come now, and let us reason together, saith the Lord; though your sins be as scarlet, they shall be as white as snow; though they be red like crimson, they shall be as wool."
—Isaiah 1:18 (KJV)

GET OUT
OF THE HOUSE!

It is very important when you have lost a loved one and are grieving to GET OUT OF THE HOUSE! For many months I would come home from work and read or just stare at the walls. For a long time, I felt as though I had no friends because no one really understood what I was going through. Those that tried to understand did not know what to say or how to treat me. Still, I do not in any way blame my friends for my suffering. I have had some very good friends through this process. I felt alone. My mom was the one I would call after games to say we won or lost and she, along with my grandmother, would be so happy. You would have thought we had won the Super Bowl. They would rejoice so much. When you lose your biggest fan and advocate, you don't know which way to turn. So, what I am saying to you is get your butt off the couch and go to a movie, take a friend to dinner, go skating . . . do something! Don't just sit around and mope.

One of the coaches I admired throughout my life was Kay Yow, the famous coach from North Carolina State University. Coach Yow died in January of 2009 from a twenty-plus year battle with breast cancer. There are two things that standout in my mind from knowing Coach Yow. The first is that when she was diagnosed with breast cancer in the 1980s, the first thing she said to her staff at North Carolina State was, "How will my parents take this?" She was more concerned about her parents' feelings than her own. She lived her life more concerned with others than herself. The other thing I won't forget about Coach Yow is her famous saying, "Don't wallow in self pity, swish your feet and get out." For those of us wallowing in self pity right now, those words are so powerful. Coach Yow said that she told herself that on the day she was diagnosed with cancer. So get up and start living. Your loved one would want you to live. I know you have heard that a thousand times and I am going make it one thousand and one times. They would not want you to suffer. They want you to live, so live life to the fullest and enjoy it. Remember the good times and move on with your life. That is what Mom wants.

CHAPTER 8

"Do not conform any longer to the pattern of this world, but be transformed by the renewing of your mind. Then you will be able to test and approve what God's will is – His good, pleasing and perfect will."
—Romans 12:2 (NIV)

A WORD
FROM THE LORD

On Saturday March 27, 2010 God gave me a Word about His Will and time. We as a people arrogantly say to God, "let Your Will be done on earth as it is in Heaven." What we don't realize is that we say it like we are *allowing* God to work on this earth. Let me tell you that God can do whatever He darn well pleases and we need to step back and accept His Will.

Even though He promised abundant living, sometimes God's Will is that we go through rough times to see the abundance and the harvest. Not many of us want to accept or believe this fact, but God must make us stronger for His purposes. We would never worship God if we did not go through pain. How can we talk about the goodness of God if we've never lost a job or loved one? Those folks who are getting drunk every night, sleeping with different people every week or those on your job who are trying to hold you back from success . . . all of these folks are crying out to God to save them from their pain. He will save you if you ask!

This time element in the Word that He gave me on Saturday is mind boggling to me because I am one of those fanatical people who can't stand to not wear a watch. I always need to know the time and to be on time and I hate it when others are not on time or waste my time. This Word was truly for me . . . the Holy Spirit revealed to me that God's time is not our time and that His time is endless. What does this mean? It means that I should stop saying that I am too old to have a baby and I should stop worrying about a husband. You see, I desperately want to get married and have children. God knows the desires of my heart and I know He will bless me, but in HIS TIME. So what if God allows me to have a child at age 50 (most women would pass out if they were told they were pregnant at age 50). He might and then He might allow me to live 20, 25 or more years to see the child raised and doing well. My God can do anything and on Saturday, I just needed a reminder of that.

CHAPTER 9

"Peace, I leave with you, my peace I give unto you: not as the world giveth, give I unto you. Let not your heart be troubled, neither let it be afraid."
—John 14:27

HER BIRTHDAY

I woke up this morning happy. Why am I happy? Today is March 31, 2010. It would have been my mother's 58th birthday and I decided to turn off my cell phone to deal with it. I was happy, as I mentioned, when I woke up until I found out how much I was paid in my final check from coaching. I made a few calls and to make a long story short, my accountant failed to tell me that I needed to claim more exemptions to get more money. Immediately my heart began to palpitate. I was not a happy camper any longer. I said a few expletives for which I repented later in the day. Then I got myself up, shook it off and went to the shower . . . on with my day I went because ultimately this was my fault.

I ate at Cracker Barrel this particular morning. Then, I went on to shop at my favorite store, Ashley Stewart. Next, I went to Charlotte to get my hair done and was back in time for Wednesday night service at church.

Let's go back to this happy phenomenon again. I woke up and was happy until the incident and then went back to being happy. Why am I happy? I lost my mother almost a year ago, today is her birthday, I have been through hell this year, I don't have a job and just received a portion of the last paycheck from my previous job (it was really more than a portion). I am happy because God has continued to shine on me and give me peace. The worst year of my life has turned into the best year of my life. "The joy of the Lord is my strength," and it is unconscionable and not understandable at all. Our small minds cannot fathom the infiniteness of God ... His timelessness ... His ubiquitousness (I know this is not a word) ... His uniqueness ... nor His wisdom without the ... **ness**. We cannot understand His love for us even though He knows we don't deserve it and that we are wicked.

He sees the depths of my soul and loves me just the same. He is the lover of my soul. What a wonderful and mighty God we serve! I wish I could explain how I feel today and how I have felt for several months now. I cannot even understand it well enough to tell you, but it is the peace and comfort of the Holy Spirit. I thought I would be a basket case on this day, but I was not.

I would like to give you some advice on how to handle a bad day. First, by all means get it out! Throw things, cry, cuss, fuss – do whatever you need to do to get it out . . . just do it alone and without ruining anyone else's day. If you have a family, go to the basement, garage or just lock yourself in the bathroom . . . DO IT BY YOURSELF! Then go on to these next steps. 2) Don't wallow in self pity. Pick yourself up, go take a shower and wash that pain away. 3) Tell the devil to leave you alone . . . he works best in your mind. 4) Pray for God's guidance, strength and wisdom. He will give it to you if you only just ask! 5) Find something to occupy your mind and time, however; don't spend your life savings occupying your time (husbands that one was for your wives! You are welcome.) 6) Don't overwhelm others with your pain, but if you need someone to talk to by all means call your best friend, sibling, pastor or parent . . . call someone who really knows you. 7) Get some exercise! It really does work and does more good for mental health than physical health (this message is not approved by the government, but is from this author's experiences). 8) Think happy thoughts and praise God for all of His blessings – the Holy Spirit will comfort you when you do this. 9) Go do something fun like dinner out or a movie. 10) If all else fails, cry some more until you feel better. I made it through this day with flying colors because of God's grace. Thank you Lord.

CHAPTER 10

"But He was wounded for our transgressions; He was bruised for our iniquities: the chastisement of our peace was upon Him; and with His stripes we are healed."
—Isaiah 53:5

UNANSWERED QUESTIONS

You know, there is not a day that goes by that I don't think of my mother. Most folks will tell you that the pain will get easier and will go away. I met a man on a plane this year who told me the pain never goes away. I thanked him for his honesty because most people just try to comfort you by telling you positive things. That is all well and good, but in order to really HEAL, you must be told the truth! The truth for me is that since my mom's death, I have thought of so many questions I want to ask her. Pardon my frankness in my next few comments, but as I write this book to help you heal, I write it to help me heal.

When you are young, you are afraid to ask your parents certain types of questions, but as you grow older, you grow bolder. My mother and I grew up together and I was hoping that we would grow old together. Back to those questions . . .

I am single, have never been married, have no children and am 40 years old. I want to ask mom how many men she loved in her life. Where was I conceived? I guess I could ask my father, but it just wouldn't be the same . . . sorry dad! If she were here, I would ask many more things. I find myself reverting back to my childhood more and more every day. I think about her often and I miss her. Some days I think I am going crazy, but I know I am not. God always swoops in to comfort me when I am having crazy thoughts. You might be having them too, but it will be alright. I want my mother! That will never go away! She will not see my children, husband or watch me walk across the stage when I receive my doctorate.

I know you are wondering while reading this, when is she going to get to the punch line? When is she going to tell me how to deal with these feelings? I want to encourage you when having these thoughts to stop and immediately think of events when you and your loved one were together. After thinking of these happy thoughts, take a deep breath and pray. Ask God to dry your tears and take away your sorrow. Then think of funny times and LAUGH! Laugh your head off! Get it out. It will make you feel better.

My mother had an incredible sense of humor. Sometimes I imagine her sitting at my kitchen table with me, my brother and my stepdad playing cards. We loved to play cards. She would be talking "smack," laughing and having an unbelievable time. Sorry Bob, but I have to tell this story . . . my mother would break out laughing uncontrollably when telling the story of how she, myself and my stepdad (Bob) were playing spades one night and he tried to "go blind." For you spades lovers, you know that you cannot do that without a partner. To this day, we all laugh about it, but only she could really tell that story. Then there was the time when she and I attended the Centennial Boule for Alpha Kappa Alpha Sorority, Inc. Specifically we were at the Centennial concert and I complained that the artist (who will go unnamed) did not perform very long for the price we paid. Very matter-of-factly, I stated, "I will never attend a Centennial concert again." My mother looked at me and said, "Crazy girl none of us will ever attend a Centennial concert again because this is the only one."

Some of those unanswered questions might be answered in your time of prayer or God may give you the knowledge to find them. Hang in there!

CHAPTER 11

"The joy of the Lord is your [MY] strength"
—Nehemiah 8:10(NIV)

MOTHER'S DAY 2010

Today is May 9, 2010 and exactly one year ago, I spoke to my mother for the last time. Many people choose to look at that as a negative, but I look at it as a positive; not just because it was on Mother's Day, but because many do not get a chance to speak to their loved ones before they pass away. At least I was blessed to do so on a special day of the year. I will cherish that memory. I am so happy today!

Now, let's jump back to yesterday . . . Yesterday was Saturday May 8th. I was fortunate enough this weekend to interview at a small and dynamic Christian school in Lakeland, FL where they are on fire for God. I enjoyed it immensely. Anyway, I had the luxury of spending part of yesterday in the Florida sun. I first relaxed alongside the pool of a grand hotel in St. Petersburg and then ventured off to the marina where I watched boats and read the final chapters of Billy Graham's book, *The Holy Spirit*. As I was reading, a strong desire came over me to put the book down and pray. My definition of prayer may be much different than yours because I talk to God incessantly. I talk to my Maker just like I would talk to you. I have a great relationship with God and can tell Him anything (even though he already knows). I believe Christians should have an attitude of prayer. Prayer is not a verb or something you do . . . it should be something you are and continuously partake in.

Anyway, I began to pray and the Holy Spirit just came over me so strongly that I started to weep uncontrollably. I was not sad! I was overwhelmed with the presence of God. I continued to pray and cry and to avoid eye contact with those passing by so they wouldn't think I was some crazy woman crying and talking to herself. The Spirit poured out on me right there in St. Petersburg and that is how it has been this entire year. This weekend, God gave me even more direction for my life and sealed in me the work that I need to be doing for His Kingdom. Thank you God for your peace and Spirit.

Back to today . . . I am happy again. As I was reading the book yesterday, Rev. Graham wrote about joy. "The joy of the Lord is my strength." This joy that I am referring to is something that only God can give. I have it and I have His peace. Neither one is exactly easy to describe or explain, but I have them both. I have not cried yet, although I know I will when I go to church, but again that will be the Spirit laying hands on me and comforting me. God also comforted me yesterday by revealing that the devil plays tricks on our minds and it causes us sadness. The devil tells you, "You should be sad today . . . why are you so happy? I declare that the devil is a liar! Don't let him trick you into sadness. Rely on God's joy, peace, grace and favor to get you through this day and every day of your life. God has been so good throughout. Happy Mother's Day!

THE FINAL CHAPTER!

"The LORD is my shepherd; I shall not want. He maketh me to lie down in green pastures: he leadeth me beside the still waters. He restoreth my soul: he leadeth me in the paths of righteousness for his name's sake."
—Psalm 23:1-3

MAY 12, 2010

Today is the one year anniversary of my mother's death and the final chapter of this book. I light a candle today in her honor as I end this book with a prayer of thanksgiving!

Dear Lord,

First, I enter Your gates with thanksgiving and thank You for waking me this morning with a new vigor, focus and renewal. Thank You Lord for this year long journey. You promised in Your Word that You would never leave us nor forsake us and You never left me this year. You have been with me every step of the way. I can't thank you enough. Thank You for the readers of this book and may it soothe their pain and give them hope. This book was not intended to make millions of dollars, but it was intended to touch lives and even if it touches only one person, it has been beneficial. Thank You for Jesus who paid the ultimate price on Calvary. He didn't have to do it but He did. He didn't have to suffer but He did. He walked on this earth fully God and fully man to take on the burdens and sins of the world. He chose to suffer and experience every pain . . . He wanted to experience the things that we experience each and every day. For this we say thank You and we can trust You because You have been there. We enter Your courts with praise! We praise You for who You are and beside You there is none other. God, You are perfect, You are holy, You are righteous, You are GOD! We hope to one day break through the veil of the Holy of Holies to see the Shekinah Glory of God. Grant it God. We plead the blood of Jesus over our lives. Give us the desires of our hearts. As I embark on this next stage of my life, give me wisdom and discernment from on high. God, You open and close doors. God, You let me know which door to walk through. God, You find that perfect job for me. God, it is Your battle. I give it to You. Bless my family today in a special way. I am not the only one remembering and hurting today. There are so many people my mother touched during her lifetime and for that I say thank You. I am still standing God. After all of the pain and suffering of this year, I am still standing. Praise Your name for that. Thank You Lord for healing. Healing has come in a miraculous way for me and although I get sad at times, the Holy Spirit swoops over me and calms my fears, removes my doubt and eases my tensions. Thank You for that. It has been so hard being motherless, even at my age. I can't imagine those who lost their mothers at an early age . . . how they must feel. There is something about being a woman in the Kingdom. We are truly blessed. I believe You put a special mechanism in us for coping and handling life's situations. I have truly been blessed by being around some amazingly strong women. Dear Lord, I cannot thank You enough or praise You enough. You are marvelous and wondrous. You are my hope. You are my peace. You are my joy. You are everything to me. Thank You for our relationship and may it flourish. May we become even more intimate. I love You God and thank You from the bottom of my heart. Peace be with all my readers. In the matchless name of Jesus I pray; Amen.

APPENDICES

Devotionals and other writings by D. Michelle Stokes for your inspiration

"It is Your Choice"

John 3:15-17, Ephesians 1:4 & 5, Hebrews 6:1-6, Matthew 6:24,25, 32-34

A familiar passage of scripture to most is John 3:16, but let's explore the verses surrounding John 3:16 . . . starting with the 15th verse. It reads, "That whosoever believeth in Him should not perish but have eternal life. For God so loved the world that He gave His only begotten Son, that whosoever believeth in Him should not perish but have everlasting life. For God sent not His Son into the world to condemn the world, but that the world, through Him, might be saved."

Ephesians 1: 4 & 5: "According as He hath chosen us in Him before the foundation of the world that we should be holy and without blame before Him in love: Having pre-destinated us unto the adoption of children by Jesus Christ to Himself, according to the good pleasure of His will."

We as humans have free choice in whom we will worship. God gave us His Son and man was given a choice of what to do with Him. We chose to crucify Him! Yes, I say we because everyday some of us crucify Him over and over again with our actions, words and deeds. To come to Christ and commune with Him is an invitation that one can accept or choose not to accept. It is up to us to decide. Once we hear the gospel, it is then up to us to make the determination. We then take on the responsibility for our actions. We can also call this invitation a gift from God. God offers this gift to us, not because we have earned it or deserve it – it is free to all . . . the gift of Salvation!

Hebrews 6: 4-6: "For it is impossible for those who were once enlightened and have tasted of the heavenly gift and were made partakers of the Holy Ghost. And have tasted the good word of God and the powers of the world to come. If they shall fall away, to renew them again unto repentance; seeing they crucify to themselves the Son of God afresh and put Him to an open shame."

Christ died for us once and there is no need for Him to die again. There is no other form of repentance needed. He paid it ALL for us. His death was sufficient and we as believers can be assured and confident in it.

Matthew 6: 24, 25, 32-34 reads: "No man can serve two masters: for either he will hate the one, and love the other; or else he will hold to the one and despise the other. Ye cannot serve God and mammon. Therefore I say unto you, take no thought for your life, what ye shall eat or what ye shall drink; nor yet for your body, what ye shall put on. Is not the life more than meat and the body than raiment? (For all these things do the Gentiles seek) for your heavenly Father knoweth that ye have need of all these things. But seek ye first the kingdom of God and His righteousness and all these things shall be added unto you. Take therefore no thought for the morrow: for the morrow shall take thought for the things of itself. Sufficient unto the day is the evil thereof."

So now it is up to you. Will you come? Will you put your trust in Him so you don't have to worry about the morrow or where you will find shelter or food or clothes or how you will pay your bills? It is your choice, whom ye will serve . . . come and give your life to Christ today! Let Him be your guide.

"HE WILL NEVER FORSAKE US"

Genesis 5:28-31, Genesis 6, 8:21,22

Noah was a descendant of Adam via Lamech. "And he called his name Noah, saying, This name shall comfort us concerning our work and toil of our hands, because of the ground which the Lord hath cursed" (Chapter 5, verse 29). The earth had gotten so corrupt and wicked that God was grieved by it, but Noah pleased God, so God wanted to protect Noah instead of punish him. We all know the story of Noah and his ark. He was told by God to build an ark 450 feet long, 75 feet wide and 45 feet high. He was also told to take two of every living creature (male and female), clean and unclean and load them up into the ark along with his family (Gen. 7: 1-5). Of course Noah obeyed God. God told him that He would send rain upon the earth for forty days and forty nights. The number forty is not used arbitrarily here. It is seen many times throughout the Bible. This number forty is used several times to signify a time of testing. Remember Noah's waiting after the tops of the mountains appeared (Gen. 8:6), or Moses' forty days on Mount Sinai in Ex. 24:18 & Deut 19:9. How about the spies' forty days searching out Canaan in Num. 13:25 or the forty years in the wilderness (Num. 14:33). This number forty is very significant in His Word.

But wait, I did not write this devotional to re-tell the story of Noah nor to talk about the significance of the number forty throughout the Bible. I wrote this to tell everyone the good news – that after this flood was over, God, realizing that man is flawed from birth and will always have a destructive heart. Genesis 8:21 - 22 says, "And the Lord smelled a sweet savor; and the Lord said in His heart, I will not again curse the ground any more for man's sake; for the imagination of man's heart is evil from his youth; neither will I again smite any more everything living, as I have done. While the earth remaineth, seedtime and harvest and cold and heat and summer and winter and day and night shall not cease." Hallelujah! This is God's covenant to us passed down through Noah. He will not forsake us and won't destroy us anymore like He did with the great flood. You can believe it and bet on it because His word shall not return to Him void. Hallelujah, Praise God!

If you keep reading the Bible, we mess up so many times and God keeps bailing us out. We are corrupt creatures and the biggest bailout came when He sent His only son to die on the cross for us. Will man ever get it? How much more does He have to sacrifice for us? Will we ever sacrifice for Him?

"WHAT SPIRIT "ARE YOU FOLLOWING?"

READ NUMBERS 14:24

Galatians 5:22-23 reads, "But the fruit of the Spirit is love, joy, peace, patience, kindness, goodness, faith, gentleness, self control. Against such things there is no law"(God's Game Plan).

Man's laws do not always jive with God's laws or Spirit. God's laws are not subject to man's laws, doctrine or acts. The fruits of the spirit . . . these are all of God. Anything that is not of God is rebellious in nature. Do you have a rebellious spirit or one of God? Are you contentious or anxious? Do you like harmony or confusion? Do you prefer positives or negatives? Is everything in your life one big mess? All things that are good, harmonious and peaceful are of God. God is not a god of confusion. He is one of harmony! God is kind, patient, loving, caring, fair and just! If we are involved in those types of things, then we are walking in His Spirit. If we are living in confusion and disharmony, then we have a rebellious spirit and one that is not of God. Check yourself to find out which spirit you are following:

1. Whatever spirit you are controlled by determines your perception! Is the glass half full or half empty? Eternal optimism is of God and of the Spirit of God. Your outlook on life is the result of the Spirit inside of you. Your outlook determines your outcome.

2. People controlled by the Spirit of God are motivated by the promises of God and not by people! We all know about

Noah and his ark, right? Noah could have thought God was crazy to tell him to build a 450 feet long, 75 feet wide and 45 feet high ark and then stock it with two of every living thing –male and female (Genesis 6:14-16). What a request! How many of us would honor such a request? Noah was sparked by the promises of God and not the rumblings of his neighbors. Only God's promises will count in the end.

3. If we walk in the Spirit of rebellion, we will not reach our full potential! God has a plan for all of our lives and an inheritance is waiting for us all. Do you want to miss out on that inheritance?

DIVINE
APPOINTMENTS

John 3:1-13 & John 4:1-26

"Nobody is too good they need not be saved and nobody is too bad they cannot be saved." Pastor in Kernersville, NC

This devotional was inspired by a sermon from a local church in Kernersville, NC. Here we have two similar stories with very different characters. In John 3, Nicodemus was a man who many would say had everything. He was wealthy. The Bible says he was a "ruler of the Jews." He was a respected religious leader and member of the Sanhedrin which governed religion and politics in Judea. Nicodemus had it all, but still needed to be born of the Spirit.

In John 4, we find the woman at the well to be an outcast. She'd had five husbands and was not married at the time she met Jesus, but did have a boyfriend that she may or may not have been living with. During those times, only the outcasts came to the well at noon (the sixth hour according to the Bible). Jesus traveled sixty miles on foot, through the mountains from Judea to Galilee and passed through a town of Samaria called Sychar. He sat down on Jacob's well to rest and that is when he met this woman.

The divine appointments between Jesus and Nicodemus and between Jesus and the woman at the well changed their lives. No one is too good or too bad that they don't need Jesus. Each of us, no matter our status in life, needs something that only the Father can provide. We search and search for answers to the mysteries of life, only to realize that the answers come through the Father. Jesus is the only answer we need!

When I was listening to the Pastor speak on this topic, he made a point to tell the congregation to look at every appointment or meeting that you have that week as a divine appointment. Nothing was going to happen by chance and God had already set up each appointment. I found that to be remarkable and that very week I had a special appointment (lunch) with some students and on that day, I remembered what the Pastor had taught me. Our lunch was not by chance, but instead, a divine appointment to do "good" in the lives of young people.

Sometimes we face obstacles when we are trying to save or help others. We might face prejudice like Jesus did when He met the woman at the well. We might have to overcome past tradition or any number of other things in order to help. As coaches and athletes we have divine appointments everyday with faculty, administration, each other . . . . Let's not forget that these are not by chance and let's make the most out of these encounters.

"The Game is Bigger than ME..."

As I was driving down the street one day (my best thoughts come at weird times, of course) a thought popped into my mind . . . "The game is bigger than ME!" It prompted me to dig a bit deeper and eventually more thoughts filled my head which led me to pen this poem:

"The game is bigger than ME...

The church is bigger than ME...

The university is bigger than ME...

The relationship is bigger than ME...

The job is bigger than ME...

Religion is bigger than ME...

The organization is bigger than ME...

Life is bigger than ME...

Learn to respect these things because it is NOT all about ME..."

First, speaking as a basketball coach, I know that many people think that coaching is so glamorous and that we only work during the season, take summers off, are greedy and make too much money. I don't blame those in the million dollar coach club (of which I am not a member) for asking for more because we are all pulled here and there and have to answer to too many. Our personal lives are often turned upside down because of the passion and drive we have. It is much more of a sacrifice than most think.

However, fellow coaches, the next time you feel you are overworked, underpaid and criticized, just find solace in knowing that the game of basketball, football, soccer . . . is bigger than you or me. The show must go on and we don't have time to feel sorry for ourselves. We must do our jobs with pride and dedication.

Speaking as a citizen and God fearing woman, wouldn't the world be a better place if everyone remembered and embraced the poem? In this microwave generation that we live in, we put ourselves above all else. If we would be selfless in our dealings with others, wouldn't the world be better off? We wonder why relationships fail. We worry too much about how we feel and not about the other person's feelings. Churches don't operate efficiently because members sit in the pews and complain and want things done like they've been done for 100 years. I could go on, but you get the point.

Now let me get off my soap box and back to being a collegiate coach. The bottom line here is that the show must go on! Life must and will keep on churning long after I am gone. This thing called LIFE is way BIGGER THAN ME!

THE POWER
TO CHOOSE

Oftentimes we take for granted the ability we have to make our own decisions in life. Authors Stephen Covey & Michael Burt wrote that there is a space between stimulus and response in which we determine (choose) how to respond. For example, the stimulus could be someone sideswiping your car at the drive-thru. Before you pull out that 9 millimeter and blow the guy's head off, shouldn't you think about the decision that should (needs to) be made in this case? We as coaches don't spend enough time contemplating which choices to make when it comes to recruiting, dealing with administrators, hiring, dealing with players, etc. We get caught up in the emotion and business of coaching. We need to make better choices and use this ability effectively. Now, going back to my original statement . . . this ability to choose is so powerful. Some would call it God's gift of freewill. It is more powerful than we can fathom & without it we are slaves to humanity. We choose when to get up from and when to go to bed. We choose whom to marry and quite often when to divorce. We choose what job or occupation to have. We choose what to wear, drive, eat and where to live. How powerful is that? In my lifetime I cannot think of too many times, even as a child, when I could not make most of the choices for my life. I cherish the idea – to CHOOSE! Let's not forget how powerful this ability is. It is a birthright, a gift, a responsibility, a privilege! Choose wisely today!

CPSIA information can be obtained at www.ICGtesting.com
Printed in the USA
LVOW081304030613

336535LV00001B/9/P

9 781450 735827